LIVES
AND
TIMES

The Wright Brothers

Margaret Hudson

Heinemann
LIBRARY

First published in Great Britain by Heinemann Library
Halley Court, Jordan Hill, Oxford OX2 8EJ,
a division of Reed Educational and Professional Publishing Ltd.
Heinemann is a registered trademark of Reed Educational & Professional Publishing Limited.

OXFORD FLORENCE PRAGUE MADRID ATHENS
MELBOURNE AUCKLAND KUALA LUMPUR SINGAPORE TOKYO
IBADAN NAIROBI KAMPALA JOHANNESBURG GABORONE
PORTSMOUTH NH (USA) CHICAGO MEXICO CITY SAO PAULO

Designed by Ken Vail Graphic Design, Cambridge
Illustrations by Roger Wade Walker
Printed in Hong Kong / China

02 01 00 99 98
10 9 8 7 6 5 4 3 2 1

ISBN 0 431 02489 8

Some words are shown in bold, **like this**. You can find out what they mean by looking in the glossary. The glossary also helps you say difficult words.

British Library Cataloguing in Publication Data

Hudson, Margaret
Wright Brothers. - (Lives & times)
1. Wright, Orville, 1871–1948 - Juvenile literature 2. Wright, Wilbur, 1867–1912 - Juvenile literature 3. Aeronautics - United States - Biography - Juvenile literature 4. Flight - History - Juvenile literature
I. Title
629.1'3'00922

Acknowledgements

The Publishers would like to thank the following for permission to reproduce photographs:

Austin J. Brown p23; Corbis-Bettmann: pp18, 19, 20; Chris Honeywell p22; Science Museum / Science and Society Picture Library p17; Wright State University Special Collections and Archives p21

Cover photograph reproduced with permission of Hulton Getty and Smithsonian Institute.

Our thanks to Betty Root for her comments in the preparation of this book.

Every effort has been made to contact copyright holders of any material reproduced in this book. Any omissions will be rectified in subsequent printings if notice is given to the Publisher.

Contents

The story of the Wright brothers................4

How can we find out
about the Wright brothers?.....................16

Glossary...24

Index..24

The first part of this book tells you the story of the Wright brothers.
The second part tells you how you can find out about their lives.

The early years

The Wright brothers were born in America. Wilbur was born in 1867. Orville was born four years later in 1871.

Wilbur and Orville always wanted to know how things worked. In 1893 they opened a shop where they made and mended bikes.

Gliders

In 1900 Wilbur and Orville began to think about how to build a machine that could fly. At first they made **models** of **gliders**. Then they found a flat, windy place to fly them.

They made the gliders big enough to
carry a person. They tried lots of ways
of making gliders. Their first one
was called *Flyer I*. It did not fly very high.

Power

In 1903 they added an **engine** to the **glider**. It made *Flyer I* heavier, but kept it up in the air. Orville took off on 17 December, 1903.

Flyer I stayed in the air for 12 seconds!
Wilbur and Orville kept on trying.
By 1905, their newest **flyer** could
stay in the air for 30 minutes.

Showing off

Everyone was excited by this new discovery. The **army** wanted to see how it worked. So did lots of other people.

Wilbur and Orville travelled round
America and Europe giving flying shows.

The company

Wilbur and Orville set up the Wright Company using the money they made from their shows.

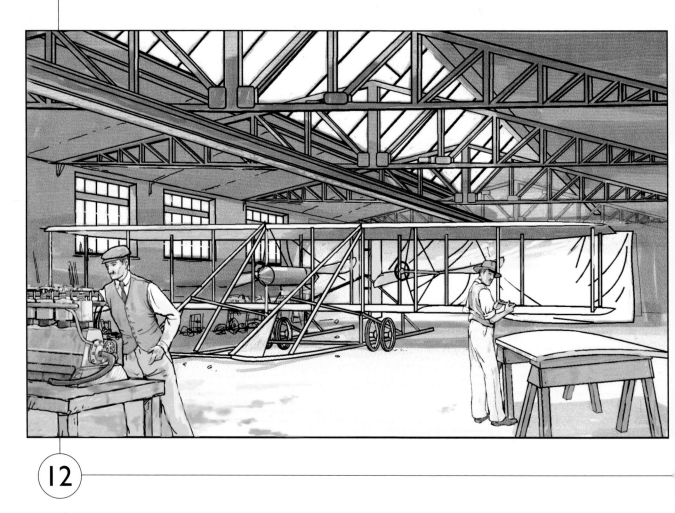

They made **flyers** to sell. They taught
people how to fly and they kept making
their flyers better and better.

Final flight

Wilbur died in 1912, aged 45. Orville went on making **flyers**, which were later renamed airplanes.

Orville's last flight was in 1918. He carried on working on his airplanes until he died in 1948, aged 77.

Clues

There are many different things from the time that tell us about Wilbur and Orville Wright.

This is an exact copy of *Flyer I*, the first **engine**-driven flying machine. It is in a **museum** in London.

Photographs

Photos show us
what Wilbur and
Orville looked like.
In this picture
they are about
40 years old.

They also show us what early flying machines were like. Can you see the pilot and the two wings?

Clues in writing

The newspapers at the time wrote about the Wright brothers and their **flyers**. This one is from 1909.

This postcard was made in Germany when Orville visited in 1909. Orville taught a German prince how to fly!

Books

Orville wrote a book called *How We Invented the Airplane*. You can still read it today.

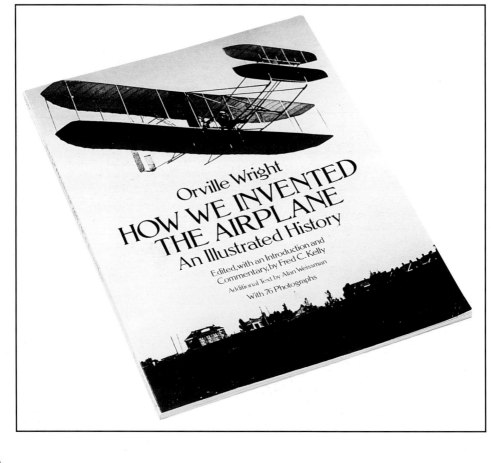

Travel

Now millions of people can travel further and faster, thanks to the Wright brothers. Today's **aeroplanes** were developed from their **flyers**.

Glossary

This glossary explains difficult words, and helps you to say words which are hard to say.

aeroplanes this is how we spell airplanes in English. You say *air-row-planes*

army the people who fight for a country

engine the machine which makes the power to push something along. You say *en-jin*

flyer the name the Wright brother gave to their flying machines

glider a flying machine that floats in the air and has no engine to push it – it is moved by the moving air around it

model small copy of something big – many models are made to work like the real big thing

museum a building which contains objects that tell us about how people lived or worked in the past

Index

airplanes 14–15
birth 4
death 14–15
flyers, early 7–9, 17, 19
     later 10–13
flying shows 11–12
gliders 6–7
jobs 5
the Wright Company 12
travel 11, 21, 23